CENTRAL AMERICA TODAY

Honduras

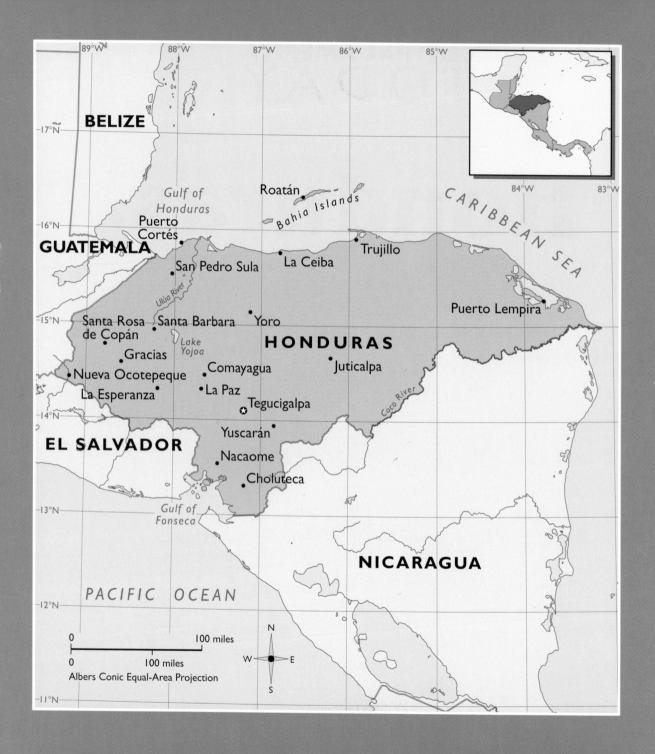

BELIZE

GUATEMALA

Gulf of Honduras

Roatán

Bahia Islands

CARIBBEAN SEA

Puerto Cortés

San Pedro Sula

La Ceiba

Trujillo

Puerto Lempira

Ulúa River

Santa Rosa de Copán

Santa Barbara

Yoro

HONDURAS

Gracias

Lake Yojoa

Comayagua

Juticalpa

Nueva Ocotepeque

La Paz

Coco River

La Esperanza

Tegucigalpa

EL SALVADOR

Yuscarán

Nacaome

Choluteca

Gulf of Fonseca

NICARAGUA

PACIFIC OCEAN

0   100 miles

0   100 miles

Albers Conic Equal-Area Projection

N
W   E
S

CENTRAL AMERICA
TODAY

Honduras

Charles J. Shields

Mason Crest Publishers
Philadelphia

Mason Crest Publishers
370 Reed Road
Broomall PA 19008
www.masoncrest.com

Printed and bound in Malaysia.

First printing

1 3 5 7 9 8 6 4 2

Library of Congress Cataloging-in-Publication Data
on file at the Library of Congress

Shields, Charles J., 1951-
  Honduras / Charles J. Shields.
      p. cm. — (Central America today)
  Includes index.
  ISBN 978-1-4222-0649-2 (hardcover) — ISBN 978-1-4222-0716-1 (pbk.)
  1. Honduras—Juvenile literature. (1. Honduras) I. Title.
  F1503.2.S56 2008
  972.83—dc22

                          2008031996

CENTRAL AMERICA
TODAY

Belize	**Guatemala**
Central America: Facts and Figures	**Honduras**
Costa Rica	**Nicaragua**
El Salvador	**Panama**

Discovering Central America

James D. Henderson

CENTRAL AMERICA is a beautiful part of the world, filled with generous and friendly people. It is also a region steeped in history, one of the first areas of the New World explored by Christopher Columbus. Central America is both close to the United States and strategically important to it. For nearly a century ships of the U.S. and the world have made good use of the Panama Canal. And for longer than that breakfast tables have been graced by the bananas and other tropical fruits that Central America produces in abundance.

Central America is closer to North America and other peoples of the world with each passing day. Globalized trade brings the region's products to world markets as never before. And there is promise that trade agreements will soon unite all nations of the Americas in a great common market. Meanwhile improved road and air links make it easy for visitors to reach Middle America. Central America's tropical flora and fauna are ever more accessible to foreign visitors having an interest in eco-tourism. Other visitors are drawn to the region's dazzling Pacific Ocean beaches, jewel-like scenery, and bustling towns and cities. And everywhere Central America's wonderful and varied peoples are outgoing and welcoming to foreign visitors.

These eight books are intended to provide complete, up-to-date information on the five countries historians call Central America (Guatemala, El Salvador, Honduras, Nicaragua, Costa Rica), as well as on Panama (technically part of South America) and Belize (technically part of North America). Each volume contains chapters on the land, history, economy, people, and cultures of the countries treated. And each country study is written in an engaging style, employing a vocabulary appropriate to young students.

A group of Nicaraguan rebels, called Contras, near their base camp in Honduras.

All volumes contain colorful illustrations, maps, and up-to-date boxed information of a statistical character, and each is accompanied by a chronology, a glossary, a bibliography, selected Internet resources, and an index. Students and teachers alike will welcome the many suggestions for individual and class projects and reports contained in each country study, and they will want to prepare the tasty traditional dishes described in each volume's recipe section.

This eight-book series is a timely and useful addition to the literature on Central America. It is designed not just to inform, but also to engage school-aged readers with this important and fascinating part of the Americas.

Let me introduce this series as author Charles J. Shields begins each volume: *¡Hola!* You are discovering Central America!

(Opposite) Thatched huts stand under palm trees on a beach in a Miskito village. The Miskito are a tribe of people who are native to Honduras. (Right) Densely packed houses in Tegucigalpa, the capital of Honduras. The city's population grew very quickly during the second half of the 20th century.

1 Honduras—The Knee of Central America

¡*HOLA!* ARE YOU DISCOVERING Honduras? It is the second-largest country in Central America after Nicaragua and is rich in natural beauty, history, culture, and hospitality. The climate ranges from the cool, mountainous interior to the warm Caribbean coastline. The attractions of this land are spectacular, including the ancient Mayan ruins of Copán; the picturesque Bay Islands in the Caribbean; the charming Caribbean coastal towns of La Ceiba, Tela, and Trujillo; the rugged beauty of the Pacific coastline; and the lush *cloud forests*, such as La Tigra. Tegucigalpa (population 1.25 million), the capital of Honduras, retains the look of *colonial* times in some neighborhoods, yet offers all the conveniences of a small city.

Honduras is the knee of Central America—bordered to the south by

Quick Facts: The Geography of Honduras

Location: Middle America, bordering the Caribbean Sea between Guatemala and Nicaragua and bordering the North Pacific Ocean between El Salvador and Nicaragua.

Geographic coordinates: 15'00" N, 86'30"W

Area: (slightly larger than Tennessee)
total: 112,090 sq. km
land: 111,890 sq. km
water: 200 sq. km

Borders: Guatemala (256 km), El Salvador (342 km), Nicaragua (922 km).

Terrain: mostly mountains in interior, narrow coastal plains.

Elevation extremes:
lowest point: Caribbean Sea 0 m
highest point: Cerro Las Minas 2,870 m

Natural resources: timber, gold, silver, copper, lead, zinc, iron ore, antimony, coal, fish, hydropower.

Land use:
arable land: 9.53 percent
permanent crops: 3.21 percent
other: 87.26 percent
Irrigated land: 800 sq. km (2003)

Source: CIA World Factbook 2008.

Nicaragua and El Salvador and on the west by Guatemala. It has a 399 mile long (644 kilometer) Caribbean coastline and a tiny 77 mile (124 km) Pacific coastline. The Caribbean Bay Islands and further northeast, the distant Swan Islands, are both part of Honduran territory.

Three-quarters of Honduras is composed of rugged hills and mountains, ranging from 984 to 9,348 feet (300 to 2,850 meters) in height. Lowlands are found only along the coasts and in major river valleys. *Deforestation* is occurring at a rate of 1,170 square miles (3,000 sq. km.) a year because of a demand for beef. Farmers cut down forests to create grassland for grazing. If this continues, Honduras will become a muddy, treeless landscape within the next 20 years. However, there are still largely untouched areas, especially in the Mosquitia region. Animals that roam the hidden regions include jaguars, armadillos, wild pigs, monkeys and alligators. Abundant bird life, such as toucans, herons and kingfishers, still can be seen, too.

The Land: Three Different Regions

Honduras has three different *topographical* regions—a large interior highland area and two narrow coastal lowlands. The interior highlands, which make up nearly 80 percent of the country's terrain, is mountainous. The mountain ranges generally run from west to east, but some valleys wander north and south, such as the large Comayagua Valley of central Honduras. The larger Caribbean lowlands in the north and the Pacific lowlands bordering the Golfo de Fonseca are mainly broad, wet plains.

Interior Highlands

The interior highlands are the chief feature of Honduran topography and are home to most of the population. However, because the rugged terrain has made both travel and farming difficult, this area has not been highly developed. The generally fertile soils, containing lava and volcanic ash, produce coffee, tobacco, wheat, corn, *sorghum*, beans, fruits, and vegetables. Farmers also raise cattle, poultry, and pigs.

In the western area of the interior highlands, Honduras's mountains blend into the mountain ranges of Guatemala. The western mountains have the highest peaks, with Pico Congolón at an elevation of 8,200 ft (2,500 m) and the Cerro de Las Minas at 9,349 ft. (2,850 m). Pine forests cover the slopes of these mountains. In the east, the mountains merge with those in

Nicaragua. Although generally not as high as the mountains near the Guatemalan border, the eastern ranges thrust up some tall peaks, such as the Montaña de la Flor, Monte El Boquerón, and Pico Bonito—all over 8,000 feet (2,439 m).

Scattered throughout the interior highlands are numerous flat-floored valleys. The floors of the large valleys provide grassland to support livestock and, in some cases, commercial agriculture. On the slopes of the valleys, farmers are able to raise only enough food to feed their families, relying on simple tools and their own hard labor. Villages and towns, including the capital, Tegucigalpa, are tucked into the larger valleys.

Vegetation in the interior highlands varies from pine forests on the western, southern, and central mountains to evergreen forests on the eastern ranges. Clinging to the highest peaks are the last patches of dense rain forest that once covered much of the highlands.

Caribbean Lowlands

The Caribbean lowlands, which most Hondurans call "the north coast," is a narrow coastal plain only a few miles wide occupying about one-fifth of the total land area of the country. Hot and humid, the Caribbean lowlands are densely forested in the interior—*lumbering* is an important economic activity. To the east and west of this section, the lowlands widen and jut into broad river valleys. The broadest river valley, along the Río Ulúa near the Guatemalan border, is Honduras's most developed sector. Two economically important places are located here—Puerto Cortés, the country's largest port, and San Pedro Sula, Honduras's industrial and agricultural center.

The afternoon sun shines through the trees in the lush cloud forest of La Tigra in the interior highlands of Honduras.

To the far east, near the Nicaraguan border, the Caribbean lowlands fan out into a humid, bug-infested area known as the Mosquitia, or the Mosquito Coast. Consisting of inland *savanna* with swamps and *mangrove*, the Mosquitia is Honduras's least developed area. During times of heavy rainfall, the few people who live here get around by shallow-draft boats. Farming and fishing are the main occupations of the scattered population.

Pacific Lowlands

The Pacific lowlands, centered on the Gulf of Fonseca, are only a small part of Honduras and contain an equally small part of the population. The land is flat, changing to swamps near the shores of the gulf. But the soil there is rich because it washes down from the mountain slopes. Farms in the Pacific lowlands produce sesame seed, cotton, and some corn and sorghum. Cattle graze in the lowland pastures, and coffee is grown on the nearby uplands. Fishing in the gulf is good for two reasons: First, the water is shallow and attracts fish and mollusks. Second, mangroves along the shore provide safe breeding grounds for shrimp and shellfish that live among the trees' roots.

Several islands in the gulf belong to Honduras. The two largest— Zacate Grande and El Tigre—are eroded volcanoes, part of the chain of volcanoes that extends along the Pacific coast of Central America. Both islands have volcanic cones that rise more than 2,296 feet (700 m). Ship captains use them as markers showing the way to Honduras's Pacific ports.

A Water-Rich Country

Honduras is a water-rich country. Numerous rivers, which have carved broad, fertile valleys, drain the interior highlands and empty to the north into the Caribbean. The downstream portions of these rivers near the Caribbean will float shallow-draft boats, but upstream from the first rapids at the foot of the mountains, only dugout canoes can be used for local travel and commerce. The major rivers in Honduras are the Ulúa, Aguán, Negro, Platano, Patuca, and, on the Nicaragua border, the Rio Coco, the largest in Central America. Economically, the most important river is the Ulúa, which flows 672 miles (400 km) through the Valle de Sula.

Rivers also define about half of Honduras's international borders. The Río Goascorán, flowing to the Golfo de Fonseca, and the Río Lempa create the border between El Salvador and Honduras. The Río Coco marks about half of the border between Nicaragua and Honduras.

Although rivers are plentiful in Honduras, large bodies of water are rare. Lago de Yojoa, located in the west-central part of the country, is the only natural lake in country. It is 37 miles (22 km) long and 23 miles across (14 km) at its widest point. Several large, muddy *lagoons* open onto the Caribbean in northeast Honduras, allowing limited transportation by boat to points along the coast.

Inside the Hurricane Belt

All of Honduras lies within the tropics, but the mountains create variety in the climate. Land below 3,280 feet (1,000 m) is commonly known as *tierra caliente* (hot land); between 3,280 and 6,560 feet (1,000 and 2,000 m) is the *tierra templada* (temperate land); and above 6,560 feet (2,000 m) is the *tierra fría* (cold land).

Each of these three main regions in Honduras has a slightly different climate. The Caribbean lowlands have a tropical, wet climate with high temperatures and humidity. Rain falls fairly regularly throughout the year here. The Pacific lowlands have a tropical, wet climate with high temperatures, too, but also a dry season from November through April. Also at that time of year, the interior highlands have a dry season, but temperatures drop as the land rises to the mountains. Overall, the interior is much cooler than the humid coast. Temperatures in the capital Tegucigalpa, for example, range between 77° and 86° F (25 and 30° C).

Honduras lies within the hurricane belt, and the Caribbean coast is especially susceptible to hurricanes or tropical storms that travel inland from the Caribbean. In 1982, Tropical Storm Alleta flooded thousands of people and caused extensive damage to crops. Hurricane Fifi killed more than 8,000 people and destroyed nearly the entire banana crop in 1974. In 1998, Honduras was hit extremely hard by Hurricane Mitch, causing loss of life in the thousands.

Plants and Animals

In eastern Honduras, the coastal and lagoon swamps have mangrove and palm forests. West of these are low, rainy, sandy plains with pine savanna, stretching inland for 40 miles (65 km) or more. Further west of the pine savanna, in low valleys and on lower moun-

Honduras is home to many types of animals, including tiny kingfishers, such as the one pictured at left perching on a bullrush, and armadillos like the one on the opposite page.

tains which are rainy all year, are broad belts of dense evergreen forests. Many species of large trees live here—mahogany, Spanish cedar, balsa, rosewood, ceiba, sapodilla, and castilloa rubber. The high, rainy mountain slopes of the Honduras highlands support excellent forests of oak and pine.

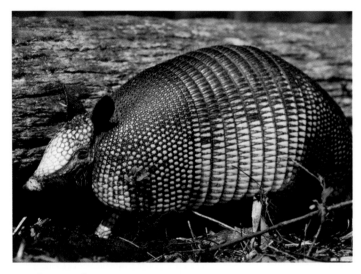

Insects, birds, and reptiles are the most often-seen creatures in Honduras. Waterfowl in large numbers inhabit the coastal areas. Crocodiles, snakes, turtles, and lizards, including giant iguana and others, are found in the tropical forest areas. Other animals include deer, peccaries, tapir, pumas, jaguars, and ocelots. Fish and mollusks are abundant in lagoons and coastal waters.

Honduras faces some serious environmental problems, however. Deforestation has led to extensive soil *erosion*. Also, *pesticides* used by banana growers have caused environmental damage in coastal regions. To safeguard native plants and animals, the Honduras government established national parks, protected forests, and biological reserves in the late 1980s and 1990s. Mount Azul de Copán National Park (established in 1987), for example, is an area of rain forest that surrounds the famous Mayan ruins of Copán. La Tigra National Park, established in 1980, covers 92 square miles (238 sq. km) of cloud forest near Tegucigalpa.

(Opposite) The devastating force of Hurricane Mitch can be seen in this aerial photograph of the piers at Guanaja, a town that was badly damaged by the 1998 hurricane. (Right) An ancient Mayan stele, or ceremonial pillar, stands under a tarp next to a stone staircase at Copán. The Maya lived in Honduras as early as 3,000 years ago.

2 Honduras Becomes the "Banana Republic"

THE HISTORY OF Honduras has been largely shaped by the land itself. Because the region is rugged, with few natural resources, Honduras has been underpopulated since ancient times. The great Indian civilizations of the time flourished primarily to the north. Later, European expeditions reported unfavorably about the land and its resources. A strong and wealthy ruling class of colonial landowners never took hold and prospered as was the case in so many other Central American countries. As a result, Honduran society today is less rigid and more *democratic* than most Central American countries.

However, Honduras's neighbors have taken advantage of the country's weaknesses to interfere in its affairs. Nations outside the region have tried to control Honduras to suit their interests. Honduras's formerly foreign-controlled economy and its United Fruit plantations, upset by periods of political unrest, gave rise to the unflattering term, "banana republic."

From the Mayans to the Colonial Period

Before the arrival of the Europeans, one of the most remarkable Indian groups in Honduras was the Maya, whose civilization spread south from the Yucatán and Guatemala. There is evidence of Maya settlement since at least 1000 B.C. at Copán in western Honduras. For three-and-a-half centuries, Copán was one of the principal centers of Mayan culture and trade. Like other Maya city-states, however, it was mysteriously abandoned around A.D. 900. The priests and rulers who built the temples, inscribed the *glyphs*, and developed the astronomy and mathematics suddenly vanished. The reason for this continues to puzzle archaeologists. Theories of civil war, disease, drought, overpopulation, and crop failure have all been suggested. Whatever the cause, the fall of the Mayan civilization seems to have affected only the city dwellers; the peasants remained in the area. Their languages and culture form links to the Mayan past.

In 1502, Columbus set foot on the American mainland for the first time at Trujillo in northern Honduras. He named the country after the deep water off the Caribbean coast—"Honduras" means "depths" in Italian, Columbus's native language.

Little exploration or settlement by Europeans took place for the two decades following Columbus' arrival. Then, Spanish *conquistadors* and a few settlers began arriving in the 1520s. Indians resisted Spanish colonialism, and, by some accounts, almost managed to drive the colonizers from the mainland. The chief of the Lenca tribe, Lempira, led 30,000 Indians against the Spanish, but he was treacherously murdered at peace talks in 1538. The Spanish crushed all Indian resistance within a year after that. The Indian population in the area dropped rapidly, almost wiped out by new diseases, mistreatment, and exportation to other colonies of large numbers of persons as slaves. By 1539, only an estimated 15,000 native people remained under Spanish control. Two years later, this figure had declined to 8,000.

Adventurers discovered gold and silver near Tegucigalpa in 1570, attracting British and Dutch pirates to the Trujillo area. Around 1600, one Spanish military leader estimated that Roatán was home to 5,000 British *buccaneers*.

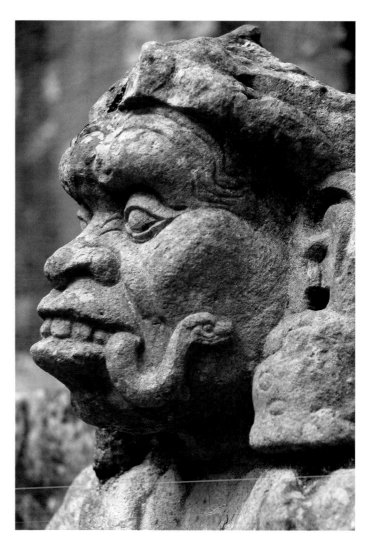

A snake crawls out of the mouth of a Mayan rain god in a stone sculpture discovered at the Copán ruins. Copán once was a center of the Mayan civilization.

By the 17th century, Honduras had become a poor and neglected backwater of the Spanish colonial empire, having a scattered population of *mestizos*—persons of mixed European and native ancestry—native people, blacks, and a handful of Spanish administrators and landowners. Raising cattle was the only important economic activity, and much of the Honduran interior and Caribbean coast remained outside Spanish control. Dutch pirates looted and burned Trujillo in 1643, and the Spanish did not resettle it until 1787.

In the early 19th century, Spanish power went into rapid decline. As Napoléon's armies marched across Europe, Spain was too deeply involved in war to pay much attention to Central America. As a result, its colonies there used the opportunity to break away as independent nations.

Independence and Strife

Spain granted independence to Honduras in 1821. Honduras briefly became part of independent Mexico, but then joined the Central American Federation in the early 1830s. But Spanish rule had fostered rivalry and suspicions among the five provinces of the federation. Constant fighting tore it apart, and in 1838, Honduras declared independence as a separate nation.

The years that followed were neither peaceful nor prosperous in Honduras. The country's weakness attracted the ambitions of individuals and nations both within and outside of Central America. The most infamous was the invasion by an American, William Walker, in 1860, whose attempt to take over Central America ended with defeat in Trujillo by an army of Hondurans, Nicaraguans, and Costa Ricans.

Even geography contributed to Honduras's misfortunes. Honduras is the only Central American republic to share land borders with three other nations: Guatemala, El Salvador, and Nicaragua. During the century and a half following Honduras's independence, civil wars throughout the *isthmus* spilled over borders. Honduran dictators tried to ally themselves with powerful neighbors, but takeovers and attempted takeovers of the government occurred frequently. The combined impact of civil strife and foreign interference kept Honduras in a state of economic and social backwardness for the next several decades.

Fruit Companies

The end of the 19th century and the first decades of the 20th century were a time of political and economic change in Honduras. The peaceful election of a president in 1899 was the first time that a legal transfer of power had taken place in decades. And in 1899, the first boatload of bananas from Honduras arrived in the United States. The fruit found a ready market here, and the trade grew rapidly. Three U.S. companies—Standard Fruit, Cuyamel Fruit, and United Fruit—eventually owned 75 percent of all Honduran banana groves. Bananas accounted for 66 percent of all Honduran exports in 1913, making the companies powerful players in the Honduran economy.

These companies became very powerful in politics as well. Until the early 20th century, the United States had played only a limited role in Honduran political clashes. But with its investments in Honduras growing, the U.S. government monitored Honduras's political scene closely. From

1920 through 1923, there were 17 uprisings or attempted *coups* in Honduras. The U.S. Navy frequently sent warships to waters near Honduras to guard American business interests. This pressure had the desired result, and more stable governments came to power from 1925 to 1931.

Political stability did not result in long-term democracy. From 1932 to 1954, two dictators ruled Honduras in turn: Tiburcio Carías Andino and Juan Manuel Gálvez. These men used harsh measures to guarantee political calm. Then, a coup ousted the elected president in 1956 and marked a turning point in Honduran history. The Honduran military had taken a hand in the overthrow and would act as an "extra government" for decades, supervising the country's politics. Over the years, however, growing economic problems made the military regime increasingly unpopular. Except for a brief period in 1969, when the country united behind the military to fight the six-day Soccer War with El Salvador, pressure slowly mounted for a return to civilian, or non-military, government.

Conflicts with Neighboring Nations

In 1969, El Salvador accused the Honduran government of mistreating El Salvadoran emigrants living in Honduras. During a World Cup-qualifying soccer match between Honduras and El Salvador, El Salvadoran troops invaded Honduran territory and bombed Honduran airports. The Soccer War, which lasted only 100 hours, soured relations between the two neighbors for the next 10 years.

The two combatants formally signed a peace treaty on October 30, 1980, which put the dispute before the International Court of Justice. In

A group of Nicaraguan Contra rebels practice with a rocket launcher at their base camp near the Honduran border. During the 1980s the Contras waged a guerrilla war against the ruling Sandinista government of Nicaragua from bases in Honduras and Costa Rica.

September 1992, the court issued a 400-page ruling, awarding much of the land in question to Honduras.

During the 1980s, turmoil in Nicaragua, El Salvador, and Guatemala troubled Honduras. Following an overthrow of Nicaragua's dictator, National Guard troops still loyal to him, known as Contras, fled into Honduras. The United States government, trying to stop *Communist* movements in Central America, poured aid and military assistance into Honduras in an effort keep it stable. In addition, the United States military provided training to the Contras and El Salvadoran refugees living in Honduran camps. When the extent of United States involvement in Central

American affairs was revealed—an estimated 12,000 Contras were operating from Honduras with American aid—anti-American demonstrations drew crowds of 60,000 in Tegucigalpa. The Honduran government finally reassessed its role as a U.S. military base, refused to sign a new military agreement with the United States, and ordered the Contras out of Honduras. With the election of a new president of Nicaragua in 1990, the war ended, and the Contras left Honduras.

Continuing Challenges

Honduras's problems remain largely economic. It is a poor country. The average annual income of Hondurans is among the lowest in the Western Hemisphere. The economy wobbles whenever banana and coffee prices drop, because

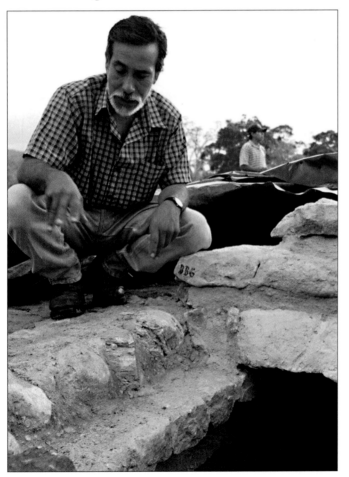

An archaeologist examines the burial site of a Mayan governor in the ancient Copán ruins in western Honduras. The grave has provided many clues about the ancient Maya.

Honduras relies so heavily on those two exports. Poor growing seasons, or too great a supply of coffee or bananas on the international market, means a drop in wages or a loss of jobs for farm workers.

About one-quarter of the total population is illiterate—in other words they cannot read or write. Less than half the population completes elementary school. Health care for the rural population—about 50 percent of the total—and much of the poor in the cities is inadequate. Aid from the United States has fallen off because Honduras no longer figures importantly in Central American politics. Given the grim social problems Honduras faces, it is surprising that the country has not seen civil unrest like the decades of fighting that wracked Guatemala.

Hurricane Mitch

In November 1998, Hurricane Mitch slammed into Honduras, hitting it the hardest of all countries in Central America. The three days of rain that followed caused landslides and floods, which buried towns and destroyed over 100 bridges throughout the country. The Río Choluteca overflowed its banks, devastating Tegucigalpa and sweeping many houses downriver. International aid and relief workers rushed to Central America to help with the recovery from the devastation. By 2000, much of Mitch's destruction had been cleared, but many of the environmental practices that contribute to flooding—clear-cutting forests, overfarming, and rapid urban expansion—continue.

(Opposite) A Honduran man carries bananas, one of the country's main export crops. About two-thirds of Hondurans are involved in banana or coffee farming. (Right) Carrying a basket of bread on her head, a woman walks past a hill that collapsed under rocks and mud in the La Colonia Soto neighborhood of Tegucigalpa.

3 A Fragile Economy

HONDURAS IS ONE OF the poorest countries in the Western Hemisphere. Since colonial times, the Honduran economy has relied on basic exports: minerals before 1900 and bananas and coffee throughout the 20th century. About two-thirds of Honduran workers are employed in agriculture. Changes in world prices for bananas and coffee affect jobs and people's livelihoods directly, and output from manufacturing remains low. Many basic problems face the economy, including rapid population growth, high unemployment, lack of farmable land, and too much dependence on coffee and bananas as exports. Honduras receives a large amount of foreign aid and technical assistance from the United States. In 1998, Hurricane Mitch, which killed more than 5,000 people, caused about $3 billion in damage.

Few Resources

Since achieving independence in 1821, Honduras has pinned its economic hopes on a handful of natural resources and on agriculture. Despite those hopes, usable land has always been severely limited due to the rugged *terrain*.

The economy is geographically divided between the interior highlands, where family farming, livestock raising, and mining have long been the main livelihoods, and the Pacific and Caribbean lowlands, where banana *plantations* employ the most workers. Food crops raised throughout Honduras include corn, beans, rice, and sugarcane, but bananas and coffee are the most important exports. Beef and seafood are exported, too. In recent years, shrimp and lobster farming have provided another important Honduran export.

During much of the 19th century, the Honduran economy did poorly. Cattle raising and family agriculture produced no major exports. In the latter part of the century, economic activity quickened with the development of large-scale, precious-metal mining. The most important mines were located in the mountains near the capital of Tegucigalpa. They were owned by the New York and Honduras Rosario Mining Company. Silver was the principal metal mined, accounting for about 55 percent of exports in the 1880s. Mining income improved the economy somewhat, but the mining industry never helped the country as a whole very much. The foreign mining companies employed a small workforce, paid little in taxes or export duties, and relied mostly on imported mining equipment.

In the first half of the 20th century, many Hondurans resented the vast banana plantations established by U.S. companies along the northern coast. In 1954, striking banana workers successfully fought for a labor code that, once drafted, became considered one of the most comprehensive in Central America. The code has generally resulted in a higher standard of living for workers and better operating conditions for businesses. Today, foreign fruit companies do not have the influence in Honduras they once did. However, labor laws are not always strictly applied, and some workplaces are substandard. Worker complaints have been especially loud in *maquiladoras*, or foreign-owned assembly plants, and in conjunction with lobster harvesting. In both cases, workers complain that their health is endangered by the conditions under which they are forced to work. Other complaints include low pay, abusive supervisors, and insufficient medical care.

An Improving Forecast

As Honduras entered the 1990s, signs that the country might be on the way to economic growth began to appear. First, a strong civilian government was able to act without interference from the military. Second, bananas were booming again, particularly as new European trade agreements created bigger markets. Small banana-producing businesses owned by workers lined up to sell their land to the commercial giants, and the last banana-producing lands held by the government were sold to private companies.

Like most of Central America, Honduras in the 1990s began to attract foreign *investors*, mostly Asian clothing assembly firms. (Look for clothes in discount stores with labels that say "Hecho en Honduras.") Burdened with a heavy national debt, aging industries, and poor roads and railroads, however, Honduras still faces economic disadvantages compared with its Central American and Caribbean neighbors, who compete with Honduras for overseas sales. Fortunately, major nations that Honduras owes money to are helping the government manage the debt and encourage more investment from abroad in new industries.

Looking ahead through the first decade of the 21st century, Honduras has only a few natural resources to use—rich pine forests and modest deposits of silver, lead, zinc, iron, gold, cadmium, antimony, and copper. But widespread slash-and-burn methods of creating farmland by

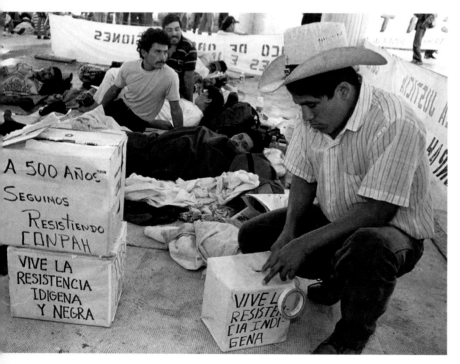

A native Honduran prepares a box he would carry on the streets of Tegucigalpa to ask for financial aid. The group of people behind him were in the seventh day of a hunger strike. They hoped to put pressure on the Honduran government to comply with agreements to give them land in their villages.

Quick Facts: The Economy of Honduras

Per capita income: $4,100; more than half the population is below the poverty line.

Natural resources: Timber, minerals, coal, fish, hydropower.

Agriculture (13.5 percent of GDP): Coffee, bananas, African palm, citrus, shrimp and lobster, sugar, tilapia, livestock.

Industry (28.1 percent of GDP*): Textiles and apparel, wood products, sugar and coffee.

Services (58.6 percent of GDP): Commerce, construction, government, banking.

Foreign trade: Exports $5.6 billion: coffee, shrimp, bananas, gold, palm oil, fruit, lobster, lumber; Imports $8.6 billion: Transport/ machinery, chemicals, industrial raw materials, fuels, foodstuffs.

Economic growth rate: 6 percent.

Currency exchange rate (2008): 18.9 lempiras = U.S. $1.

* GDP or gross domestic product—the total value of goods and services produced in a year.   Source: CIA World Factbook 2008

destroying forests continue, and mineral exports are hampered by inadequate road and rail systems—most roads are unpaved. Industry, located chiefly in San Pedro Sula, is small and produces goods for local markets: processed food (mainly sugar and coffee), textiles, clothing, lumber, and wood products. On the other hand the Honduran maquiladoras grow stronger all the time, providing employment to 100,000 workers in 2002 and generating more than $330 million in foreign exchange for the country.

Tourism also has great potential for generating income in Honduras. The clear, warm Caribbean waters are ideal for sport diving, and the coral-sand beaches and climate attract international vacationers. The famous Mayan ruins at Copán and the well-preserved colonial fort at Omoa also attract thousands of visitors each year.

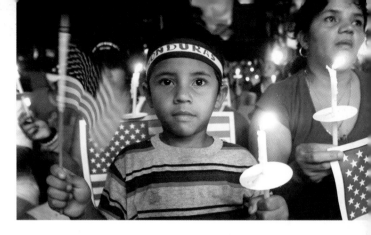

(Opposite) Tobacco plantation workers take a break in the shade of a grass-roofed hut. (Right) A four-year-old Honduran boy holds a candle and flag at a prayer service in the wake of the September 11, 2001, terrorist attack that destroyed the World Trade Center in New York City and damaged the Pentagon in Washington, D.C.

4 The People of Honduras

AMONG THEMSELVES, Hondurans are known affectionately as *catrachos*. About 90 percent of the population are *mestizos*—Spanish-speaking persons of Indian-Spanish heritage. Most of the Indians are Lenca. They are found in the southwest, near the Guatemala border, close to the important Indian centers of the Mayan period. More than 100 years ago, immigrants from the Caribbean Islands settled in the lowlands and the Bay Islands. These are the Garifuna, or Black Caribs, who live in 44 coastal villages. Then, in the 1970s and 1980s, a new population—approximately 50,000 refugees—arrived in Honduras to escape the civil unrest in surrounding countries. Most are housed by the United Nations in camps near the borders, but numerous uncounted illegal refugees are scattered throughout the country.

Population Growth

Generally, the population of Honduras is concentrated in the interior highlands and in the Caribbean lowlands. Almost two-thirds of Hondurans live in rural areas. The largest urban centers are the capital, Tegucigalpa; San Pedro Sula, the center of industry and agriculture; La Ceiba, home of the former Standard Fruit Company; and Choluteca.

The population grew extremely fast during the mid-20th century posing a big problem in employment and housing. During the 1980s and 1990s, there was an especially rapid increase in urban population in and around Tegucigalpa, causing overcrowding in housing and air and water pollution. Although the rate of population growth in Honduras slowed by the late 1990s, it remained well above the world average. In the rest of the country, the mountainous, forested terrain and dirt roads isolate the rural poor.

Rural Life

Honduras is still one of the least urbanized countries of Central America. Rural residents are farmers, although about 60 percent of Honduran land remains covered with forest. Only 25 percent of the total land is available for agriculture or pastureland.

A vast majority of rural dwellers are small farmers who till their own plots or landless laborers who work for wages on estates or smaller farms. The move toward small farms increased rapidly after 1960 as the population grew. Because the peasants divided their land among all the sons, a farmer with six sons will divide an already-small farm six ways. Many peasants with plots of their own also seek part-time jobs to increase their incomes. For example, a man may work his father's land, rent additional land of his own, and do occasional day labor, too.

The steepness of the mountain slopes often makes agriculture impossible or at least extremely hard. It is estimated that almost 90 percent of the mountainous area of Honduras has slopes that barely support farming or even grassland for animals. In addition, exhausted or poor soil and crop losses result in poverty for small farmers.

Part of the soil erosion and loss of soil fertility comes from the methods used in farming. To clear land, small farmers tend to use the slash-and-burn method. This consists of hacking down vegetation with *machetes* and then burning it. Using hoes, axes, digging sticks, and possibly wooden plows, they plant the ground without the use of fertilizer. A percentage of the harvest then ends up ruined because it is stored in unprotected facilities and eaten by rodents and pests.

Did You Know?

- Honduras has a democratic constitutional government. Its current constitution became effective on January 20, 1982. It was amended in 1995.
- The president is elected by popular vote to a four-year term. In 2006, Manuel Zelaya Rosales was elected president of Honduras.
- There are 128 seats in Honduras's National Congress or *Congreso Nacional*. Members are elected by popular vote to serve four-year terms).
- The Supreme Court of Justice or *Corte Suprema de Justicia* consists of judges elected for four-year terms by the National Congress.
- Major political parties in Honduras include the Liberal Party (PLH), National Party of Honduras (PNH), National Innovation and Unity Party (PINU), and the Christian Democratic Party (PDCH).
- The capital of Honduras is Tegucigalpa.
- The voting age is 18.

A Honduran farmer burns land in preparation for the second half of the planting season in August 2001. This farmer, who lives outside the village of La Concepción, intends to plant corn and beans once the fields have been cleared.

Most of the rural people live in one- or two-room thatch-roofed huts (*bahareques*) built of adobe or sugarcane stalks and mud with dirt floors. The size of plantations and commercial cattle farms has grown in the last few decades, making it harder for peasants to find a plot of land suitable for a house. Many who once lived on the edges of larger estates were forced off the land. As a result, there is much "fence housing" in Honduras. A *squatter* and his family, squeezed off land by plantation crops, live in a tiny hut in the narrow space between a public road and the landowner's fence.

Living in poverty, most of the rural people exist on a plain but not very nutritious diet: corn tortillas, beans, cassava melons, plantains, rice, and coffee. Each rural household usually has pigs and chicken, but meat doesn't appear on the table very often, nor do green vegetables for that matter.

In fact, food production in Honduras has never been equal to the people's needs. Widespread *malnutrition* contributes to the population's fragile health. Although the food supply is just enough to subsist, it is not sufficient to promote good health. Hondurans often do not link infectious diseases, low birth weights, or mental retardation with poor diet and lack

Quick Facts: The People of Honduras

Population: 7,639,327

Ethnic groups: 90 percent *mestizo* (mixed Indian and European); 7 percent Amerindian; 2 percent black; 1 percent white.

Age structure:
    0–14 years: 38.7 percent
    15–64 years: 57.8 percent
    65 years and over: 3.5 percent

Population growth rate: 2.024 percent

Birth rate: 26.93 births/1,000 population

Infant mortality rate: 24.61 deaths/1,000 live births

Death rate: 5.36 deaths/1,000 population

Life expectancy at birth:
    total population: 69.37 years
    male: 67.81 years
    female: 71.01 years

Total fertility rate: 3.38 children born per woman.

Religions: 97 percent Roman Catholic; 3 percent Protestant or Indian beliefs.

Languages: Spanish and Amerindian dialects.

Literacy: 80 percent (2001 est.)

*All figures 2008 estimates, unless otherwise noted.   Source: CIA World Factbook 2008

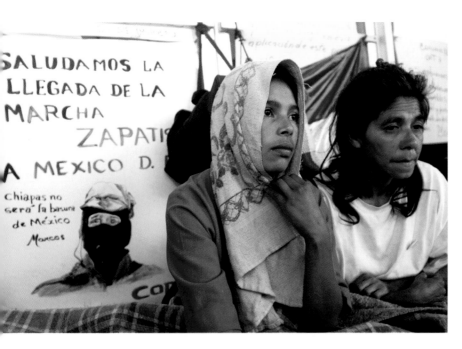

Two members of the native Lenca tribe participate in a hunger strike in front of the Honduran Supreme Court in March 2001. They were protesting the arrest of eight tribe members who claimed that their civil rights had been violated.

of sanitation. These problems have always existed in people's memories, so they tend to be accepted as normal.

Urban Life

Urban life in Honduras, as in many developing countries, points up the contrasts between the lifestyles of the well-off and the poor. Tegucigalpa and San Pedro Sula offer blocks of elegant apparel shops and jewelry stores. Tall office buildings provide headquarters for business and professional people who make up the rather small middle- and upper classes.

For most of Tegucigalpa's urban population, however, living conditions aren't much better than those of the rural poor. Unskilled job seekers coming to Tegucigalpa usually settle in the slums of the city center. When neighborhoods become too crowded, the slums, or *barrios*, creep outward toward the edges of the city. *Barrio* residents live in *cuarteríos*—unsanitary rows of windowless, dirt-floored rooms. The average household in the poor sections of cities often contains about seven persons in a single room, although sometimes a small kitchen stands in the rear covered by a tile overhang. Some *cuarterías* face the street, while others are arranged in double rows facing each other across a block-long alley, barely wide enough for a person to walk through. For those living in the rooms facing an alley, the narrow passageway between buildings serves both as a sewage and waste disposal area and as a courtyard for as many as 150 persons.

Relatives and friends tend to cluster together in the *barrios*, offering support to one another. But the pressures of poverty cause families to break apart, too. High unemployment forces parents to take migratory laboring jobs, moving around from place to place. Fathers desert their families, leaving the care and support of children entirely to mothers. Some children are abandoned to live on the streets. Beggar children haunt the airport in Tegucigalpa, for instance, rummaging through garbage and offering to carry tourists' luggage for tips.

The diet of the poor in the cities is only a little better than that of the rural poor, although open-air markets offer a greater variety of food. Many of the Hondurans who leave the country in search of work wind up in the United States, either as legal or illegal immigrants.

(Opposite) Honduran soccer player Carlos Pavón, wearing the blue-and-white shirt, dives for the ball during a World Cup qualifying match at Honduras's Olimpico Metropolitano Stadium in San Pedro Sula. Soccer is the favorite sport of many people of Honduras. (Right) Lime adds an accent to the food served at this traditional meal in Honduras.

5 Language, Religion, and Home Life

LANGUAGE, RELIGION, AND home life are the three central elements of Honduran culture. Spanish is the main language spoken throughout Honduras, although English is the language of choice in the Caribbean Islands. Most Hondurans are Roman Catholic, although there are many other churches, too, including Mormons, Jehovah's Witnesses, Seventh Day Adventists, Baptists, Pentecostals, Assemblies of God, and Evangelicals. Native Indian groups have their own religions, often blending elements of African and Indian ancestor-worship with Christian practices. Finally, the family is central to Honduran daily life and society, and strong emphasis is placed on family loyalty.

Signs of the Past

Any visitor to Honduras will notice that the art and architecture of the Mayan and Spanish colonial periods are strongly evident in Honduran culture. Of special interest to tourists, archeologists, and historians is the great Mayan city of Copán, which represents the height of the Mayan Classic period. Discovered in the early 16th century, Copán was partly excavated and restored in 1839. Spanish architecture in Honduras also reflects styles borrowed from 16th–18th century southern Europe.

Modern Honduran culture has not produced many examples of its own art, mainly because of the country's widespread poverty. Most artists re-create their Spanish heritage, and the Mayan past is seen chiefly in Indian crafts.

The Influence of the Catholic Church

The Roman Catholic Church has been a powerful institution in Honduras since colonial times. In the 1880s, the Honduran government tried to reduce the influence of the Roman Catholic Church by stripping it of some of its economic and political power. Nevertheless, in the 20th century the church actually enlarged its role in Honduran affairs, especially in regard to the rights of the poor.

In the 1950s, the Roman Catholic Church in Honduras launched a campaign to encourage church membership. During the 1960s and 1970s, local priests became outspoken critics of the military and the government's treatment of the poor. The tension reached a terrible pitch in 1975, when

In La Esperanza, traditional dancers take part in a celebration—a mock trial of Christopher Columbus, who is accused of destroying the native culture of Honduras.

landowners in Olancho murdered 10 peasants, two students, and two priests for organizing protests over land ownership and the wages paid to agricultural workers After this incident, the government took measures to stop the criticism. Expulsions and arrests of foreign priests took place, and

Hundreds of devoted Catholics participate in the midnight Procession of Silence, held in Tegucigalpa on Good Friday every year. The procession marks Jesus Christ's silent walk from the Last Supper to the Mount of Olives. The population of Honduras is almost entirely Roman Catholic, although the number of Protestant Christians is growing.

some church-sponsored peasant centers were forced to close. The Roman Catholic Church retreated temporarily, but renewed its calls for reform in the 1980s.

As a result, Protestant churches underwent a tremendous growth in membership during the 1980s. The largest numbers are found in Methodist, Church of God, Seventh Day Adventist, and Assemblies of God denominations. These churches sponsor social service programs in many communities, making them attractive to the poor.

Today, all church schools receive government funding, and religious instruction is part of the public school curriculum.

The Importance of the Family

The family is central to Honduran daily life and society. Family ties contribute to Hondurans' identity, and relatives help one another in business. Some family members add to the household income by learning crafts: woodcarving (notably wooden instruments), basketry, embroidery and textile arts, leather craft, and ceramics. These are sold on market days or in tourist areas.

Hondurans usually marry in religious ceremonies, but civil marriages performed by a judge are common, too. Many couples live together until they can afford a religious ceremony and a wedding celebration. Close, trusted friends are often brought into family circles by being designated *compadres* (godparents), an honor—and a responsibility—that is often given at marriages and baptisms.

In Honduran households, the meals are based around beans, rice, tortillas, fried bananas, meat, potatoes, cream, and cheese. Celebrations bring out specialty dishes, such as tamales and *yuca con chicharrón* (fried cassava and pork). There are also many *comidas típicas* (typical foods)

Did You Know?

Honduras's flag consists of three equal horizontal bands of blue (top), white, and blue with five blue five-pointed stars arranged in an X pattern centered in the white band. The stars represent the members of the former Federal Republic of Central America—Costa Rica, El Salvador, Guatemala, Honduras, and Nicaragua.

special to various regions of the country, including *sopa de hombre* (man's soup) and seafood dishes in the south, *queso con chile* (cheese with chili peppers) in the west, and *cazabe* (mashed cassava) among Garifuna or Black Caribs in the Caribbean lowlands.

The gap between the wealthy (and even the middle class) and the poor is wide, especially in regards to food. The poor tend to rely on corn, often eaten as tortillas. Beans, cassava, plantains, and rice are common, but meat and green vegetables are not. Poor families in rural areas typically live on tiny parcels of land, and urban poor often live in cramped, unsanitary rows of dirt-floored rooms called *cuarterías*.

Recreation and Sports

Hondurans listen to several radio stations featuring rock and popular music from the United States and Europe. Televisions are not common— there are just 29 television sets for every 1,000 people in the country. Many television programs are imported and dubbed into Spanish, and motion pictures are usually Hollywood imports with Spanish subtitles. Family recreation often revolves around religious festivals honoring local saints. On February 3, for example, Catholics throughout the nation celebrate the patron saint of Honduras, the Virgin of Suyapa, named for the village near which her image was found.

Soccer is a passion of many Hondurans. There is hardly a village that does not sponsor a team or club at some level of competition. International matches attract the whole country's attention. In 1998, the Honduran national team advanced to the semifinals in the 1998 World Cup, and the squad took second place at the 1999 Pan American Games after defeating the United States, Uruguay, Cuba, Jamaica, and Canada.

Honduras's better-quality sports and recreational facilities are used mainly by tourists. Scuba diving, swimming, and sport fishing are popular in the resort region around Cannon Island, on the northern coast.

Cultural Institutions and Newspapers

Cultural institutions in Honduras include the National School of Music and the Republican History Museum, both in Tegucigalpa, and the Archaeological Museum of Comayagua. The Autonomous National University of Honduras, founded in 1847 in Tegucigalpa, enrolls more than 30,000 students. Small theaters produce plays in both Spanish and English.

There is general freedom of the press in Honduras, and daily newspapers are published in the principal cities of the country. The newspapers of Tegucigalpa and San Pedro Sula are the widest read, and several have Internet editions.

Honduran Festivals

There are festivities in just about every town to celebrate saints' days. The fair for the Virgen de Suyapa, patron saint of Honduras, is celebrated in Suyapa, 4 miles southeast of Tegucigalpa, during the first two weeks of February. Because of the number of Roman Catholics in the country, important celebrations revolve around such religious holidays as Christmas, the season of Lent, Holy Week, and Easter.

Other public holidays include New Year's Day (January 1), Panamerican Day (April 14), Labor Day (May 1), Independence Day (September 15), Francisco Morazán Day (October), Columbus Day (October 12), and Army Day (October 21).

Carnaval at La Ceiba is celebrated during the third week of May with parades, costumes, and street music. There are other popular fairs in Copán Ruinas (March 15–20), Tela (June 13), Trujillo (June 24), San Pedro Sula (last week in June), and Danlí (the last weekend in August).

The Feria Centroamericana de Turismo y Artesanía, a Central American international artisans' and tourism fair, is held annually from December 6–16 in Tegucigalpa. Another cultural fair is held in Copán Ruins from December 15–21.

A school marching band performs during Independence Day festivities. Hondurans celebrate September 15 as the date Central America received its independence from Spain, although related festivities continue throughout the month.

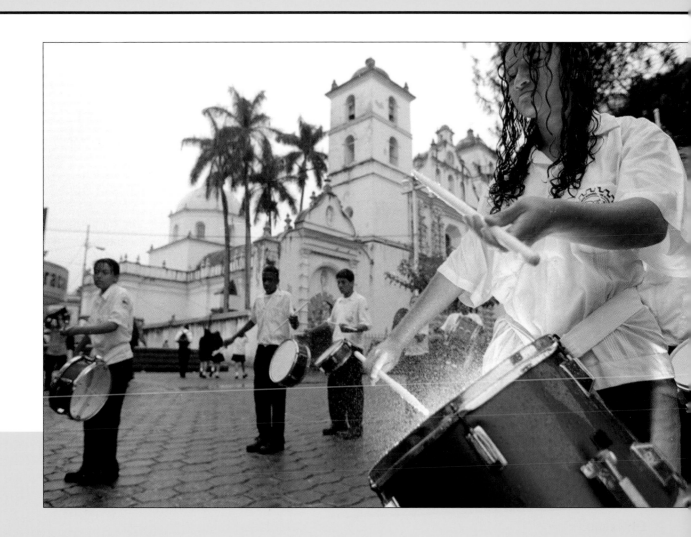

Recipes

Dulce de Leche

(Serves 3 to 4)
1 quart milk
1 cup sugar
1 tsp. vanilla
6 slices of white bread, torn into tiny pieces
2 egg yolks, beaten
Cinnamon to taste

Directions:
1. Cook the milk together with the sugar, vanilla, and cinnamon, and stir constantly.
2. When milk begins to thicken, add bread, and continue stirring.
3. When mixture gets thick, remove from heat, and beat thoroughly. While it is still warm, add the well-beaten egg yolks, and let the batch cool.
4. Refrigerate until ready to eat.

Guacamole

1 cup mashed avocado
1/4 cup mayonnaise
2 Tbs. lemon juice
1/4 cup finely chopped stuffed olives
1 Tbs. grated onion
1 tsp. salt
1/4 tsp. chili powder or cayenne
12 oz. bag of tortilla chips

Directions:
Combine mashed avocado, mayonnaise, lemon juice, olives, onion, and seasonings. Chill.
Use as a dip for the chips.

Plantain Pancakes

(Serves 3 to 5)
3 very ripe plantains
3 Tbsp. flour
4 Tbsp. melted butter
2/3 cup cooked red kidney beans
2/3 cup shortening

Directions:
1. Boil and mash plantains. Add flour and butter, and mix thoroughly.
2. Fry the beans in 1 Tbsp. shortening for about 5 minutes.
3. Heat remaining shortening in another frying pan. Add plantain mixture, 1 Tbsp. at a time, and spread with a fork so that it will take the shape of a small pancake. Fry the pancakes for about 5 minutes. Place a teaspoon of the fried beans on each, and fold.
4. Fry the stuffed pancakes, covered, three minutes on each side or until brown.

Coconut Bread

(Serves 6 to 8)
1 lb. shredded coconut
3 cups all-purpose flour
1 Tbsp. baking powder
1/2 cup butter
1 cup sugar
2 eggs
2 tsp. salt

Directions:

1. Preheat oven to 350° F.
2. Mix dry ingredients in a large bowl.
3. Beat eggs and add to dry ingredients. Add melted butter.
4. Mix ingredients together. Add a little milk if the batch seems dry.
5. Pour into two lightly greased loaf pans or two lightly greased pie dishes.
6. Bake for about 40-45 minutes or until toothpick comes out clean from the center.

Rompopo (Honduran Eggnog)

(Serves 8 to 10)
1/2 gallon milk
8 egg yolks
1/4 cup sugar
3 large cinnamon sticks
2 cloves
Dash of pepper
1 cup white grape juice
Pinch of nutmeg

Directions:

1. In a big pot, boil milk together with sugar, cinnamon, nutmeg, and cloves.
2. In a bowl, separate yolks and whites, and beat the yolks.
3. Cook milk and yolks at medium heat, stirring constantly until the mixture loses its egg flavor. Let it cool, and add grape juice
4. Keep eggnog in a covered bowl, and refrigerate.
5. Do not add ice when serving eggnog.

Glossary

Buccaneer—a pirate who preyed on Spanish colonies and shipping in the Caribbean region during the 17th century.

Cloud forest—a wet, tropical forest that has clouds surrounding it even in the dry season.

Colonial—having to do with one country using the resources of another.

Communist—a political system in which all resources are distributed by a central authority.

Conquistadors—Spanish conquerors of the late 16th century.

Coup—the violent overthrow of an existing government by a small group.

Deforestation—the action or process of clearing forests.

Democratic—characterized by free and equal participation in government or in the decision-making processes of an organization or group.

Erosion—the act of wearing away, usually dirt or rocks.

Glyphs—pictures carved in stone that tell stories.

Investors—person who puts money into a business.

Isthmus—narrow stretch of land with water on two sides.

Lagoon—a coastal body of shallow water formed where low-lying rock, sand, or coral presents a partial barrier to the open sea.

Lumbering—to cut down the trees in a region and convert them into saleable lumber.

Machete—a large, heavy broad-bladed knife used as a tool for cutting through vegetation.

54

Malnutrition—poor health and low weight caused by lack of food.

Mangrove—tropical tree that has an extensive root system and is important to land-building.

Maquiladoras—foreign-owned assembly plants.

Pesticide—a chemical substance used to kill pests, especially insects.

Plantation—a large estate or farm, usually worked by resident laborers.

Savanna—a flat grassland, sometimes with scattered trees, in a tropical or subtropical region.

Sorghum—a cereal plant that is resistant to drought, widely cultivated in tropical and warm areas as a grain crop and for animal feed.

Squatter—a person who settles on property that he or she does not own and has no title to.

Terrain—physical features of a tract of land.

Topographical—how land is shown on maps.

Project and Report Ideas

Maps

- Using a heavy piece of cardboard or poster board, first draw a large map of Honduras. Then, using a mixture of flour and paste, create three-dimensional mountain ranges. Refer to a topographical map that appears in an encyclopedia as a guide. Use watercolors to paint the mountain ranges when you're finished—be sure to label the ranges.
- Use a physical map of the United States or the world to locate states or countries with physical features similar to those of Honduras. Would the climate and lifestyle (food, clothing, leisure activities, livelihoods, etc.) of those areas be the same as that of Honduras? Why or why not?
- Locate and research the lifestyles of people living in various mountain regions around the world. Create a poster showing how people in mountainous regions share similar traits.
- Work in a small group to research the climate, resources, and cultures of cities in the United States that are at the same altitude as Tegucigalpa.
- Draw a large map of Honduras. Leave room in the margins to write one-paragraph descriptions of jungle or forest animals that live in Honduras. Draw or cut out pictures of these animals to go with your descriptions.

Flashcards

Using the glossary in this book, create flashcards. Put the term on one side and the definition on the other. Practice with the cards in pairs. Then, choose two teams of three. Select a referee to say the term out loud, and then call on someone to give the definition. The referee's decision is final. Award points for each correct answer. You can also read the definition, and ask for the correct term instead!

Short Reports

- Respond in writing to one or both of these questions: What is a rain forest? What does a rain forest have to do with me?
- Research the location and problems of rain forests in the United States. Compare the problems of deforestation in U.S. rain forests with the problems of deforestation in Honduras.
- Write a one-page report on Hurricane Mitch, which hit Honduras in 1998.
- Write a short report on the contras: Who were they? Why did the United States support them?
- Write a short report on William Walker: Who was he? Why was he trying to take over Central America?

Projects

- Using a picture of a Mayan temple, build a small-scale model or show what Copán looks like from the air.
- Using the same picture, re-create a Mayan glyph using model clay. Make it about the size of a textbook lying flat.

Chronology

1000 B.C.	The Maya settle at Copán in western Honduras.
A.D. 600–900	Mayan culture is at its strongest.
1502	Columbus sets foot on the American mainland for the first time at Trujillo in northern Honduras; he names the country after the deep water off the Caribbean coast.
1520	Spanish conquistadors and a few settlers begin arriving.
1538	Chief of the Lenca tribe, Lempira, who is leading 30,000 Indians against the Spanish, is murdered during peace talks.
1570	Adventurers discover gold and silver near Tegucigalpa.
1643	Dutch pirates loot and burn Trujillo.
1821	Spain grants independence to Honduras.
1860	American adventurer, William Walker, who attempts to take over Central America, is defeated in Trujillo by an army of Hondurans, Nicaraguans, and Costa Ricans.
1920–1923	Seventeen uprisings or attempted government overthrows in Honduras give rise to the term "banana republic."
1932–1954	Honduras is ruled by two dictators: Tiburcio Carías Andino and Juan Manuel Gálvez.
1956	The military ousts the president of Honduras. It will continue to manage Honduran politics for decades.
1969	Six-day Soccer War with El Salvador over alleged mistreatment of El Salvadoran immigrants in Honduras.

1980	Honduran refugee camps serve as military training grounds for U.S.-aided troops fighting Communist-supported governments in surrounding countries; the Contras become a major political issue in the United States.
1980–1990	To safeguard native plants and animals, the Honduras government establishes national parks, protected forests, and biological reserves.
1998	Hurricane Mitch slams into Honduras, killing 5,000 people and causing $3 billion in damage.
2002	Newly elected president Ricardo Maduro takes office in January.
2003	Although much of Hurricane Mitch's destruction has been repaired, Honduras remains the poorest country in Central America.
2004	In August, Honduras tightens security at foreign embassies and declares a national terror alert after receiving information that al-Qaeda is trying to recruit Hondurans to attack embassies of the United States, Britain, Spain, and El Salvador.
2006	Manuel Zelaya begins a four-year term as president of Honduras in January.
2008	The Honduran government joins the Bolivarian Alternative for the People of Our America (ALBA), an international organization that also includes Venezuela, Cuba, Nicaragua, Bolivia, and Dominica.

Further Reading/Internet Resources

Chandler, Gary, and Liza Prado. *Honduras and the Bay Islands*. Oakland, Calif.: Lonely Planet, 2007.

Dedlinger, Roger E. *Honduras*. New York: Chelsea House, 2008.

Foster, Lynn V. *A Brief History of Central America*. New York: Checkmark Books, 2007.

Hall, Diane, ed. *Celebrate in Central America*. New York: Lothrop Lee & Shepard, 1997.

Henderson, James D., et al, editors. *A Reference Guide to Latin American History*. Armonk, N.Y.: M.E. Sharpe, 2000.

Kras, Sara Louise. *Honduras*. New York: Scholastic, 2006.

Woodward, Ralph Lee Jr. *Central America: A Nation Divided*, 3rd ed. New York: Oxford University Press, 1999.

History and Geography

http://www.britannica.com/eb/article?eu=118721
http://memory.loc.gov/frd/cs/hntoc.html#hn0004

Economic and Political Information

http://www.state.gov/www/background_notes/honduras_1099_bgn.html
https://www.cia.gov/cia/publications/factbook/geos/ho.html

Travel, Culture, and Festivals

http://www.infoplease.com/ipa/A0107616.html
http://www.honduras.com/

American Chamber of Commerce
Hotel Honduras Maya
Apartado Postal 1838
Tegucigalpa, Honduras
(504) 232-7043/232-6035

American Field Service (AFS) Honduras
Colonia El Castaño
Avenida Los Castaños
Casa 2941
Apartado Postal 1300
Tegucigalpa, Honduras
(504) 232-7670
www.afs.org/partners/honhome.htm

Caribbean/Latin American Action
1818 N Street, N.W.
Suite 310
Washington, D.C. 20036
(202) 466-7464
www.claa.org

Embassy of Honduras
3007 Tilden Street, N.W.
Washington, D.C. 20008

Friends of Honduras
7033 S.E. Mitchell Street
Portland, Oregon 97206

Honduras Institute of Tourism
2100 Ponce de Leon Blvd, Suite 1175
Coral Gables, FL 33134
(305) 461-1601

The American School
Tegucigalpa, Honduras
(504) 239-3333
info@amschool.org
www.amschool.org

U.S. Department of Commerce
International Trade Administration
Office of Latin America and the Caribbean
14th and Constitution Avenue, N.W.
Washington, D.C. 20230
(202) 482-0057
800-USA-TRADE
www.ita.doc.gov

U.S. Agency for International Development
1300 Pennsylvania Avenue, N.W.
Washington, D.C. 20523-0001
(202) 712-4810

Index

Index/Picture Credits

Contributors

Senior Consulting Editor **James D. Henderson** is professor of international studies at Coastal Carolina University. He is the author of *Conservative Thought in Twentieth Century Latin America: The Ideals of Laureano Gómez* (1988; Spanish edition *Las ideas de Laureano Gómez* published in 1985); *When Colombia Bled: A History of the Violence in Tolima* (1985; Spanish edition *Cuando Colombia se desangró, una historia de la Violencia en metrópoli y provincia*, 1984); and co-author of *A Reference Guide to Latin American History* (2000) and *Ten Notable Women of Latin America* (1978).

Mr. Henderson earned a bachelors degree in history from Centenary College of Louisiana, and a masters degree in history from the University of Arizona. He then spent three years in the Peace Corps, serving in Colombia, before earning his doctorate in Latin American history in 1972 at Texas Christian University.

Charles J. Shields, the author of all eight books in the DISCOVERING CENTRAL AMERICA series, lives in Homewood, a suburb of Chicago, with his wife Guadalupe, an elementary-school principal. He has a degree in history from the University of Illinois in Urbana-Champaign, and was chairman of the English department and the guidance department at Homewood-Flossmoor High School in Flossmoor, Illinois.